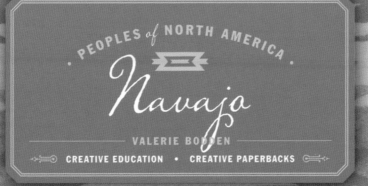

· PEOPLES *of* NORTH AMERICA ·

Navajo

VALERIE BODDEN

CREATIVE EDUCATION · CREATIVE PAPERBACKS

Published by Creative Education and Creative Paperbacks
P.O. Box 227, Mankato, Minnesota 56002
Creative Education and Creative Paperbacks
are imprints of The Creative Company
www.thecreativecompany.us

Design and production by Christine Vanderbeek
Art direction by Rita Marshall
Printed in Malaysia

Photographs by Alamy (CH Collection, Chris Howes/Wild Places Photography, George H.H.
Huey), Corbis (Bettmann, Christie's Images, Corbis, P. G. Gates/National Geographic Society,
Hulton-Deutsch Collection, Lake County Museum, Danny Lehman, Jim McHugh/Sygma,
Ted Spiegel, Marilyn Angel Wynn/Nativestock Pictures), iStockphoto (belfasteileen, foofie,
ivanastar, johnaudrey, karenfoleyphotography, lucky-photographer, Peter Mukherjee,
samdiesel, tobkatrina), Shutterstock (Don Mammoser, OHishiapply, Denis Tabler, Transia Design)

Library of Congress Cataloging-in-Publication Data
Bodden, Valerie.
Navajo / Valerie Bodden.
p. cm. — (Peoples of North America) • Includes bibliographical references and index.
Summary: A history of the people and events that influenced the North American Indian
tribe known as the Navajo, including headman Manuelito and conflicts such as the Second
Battle of Fort Defiance.
ISBN 978-1-60818-553-5 (hardcover)
ISBN 978-1-62832-154-8 (pbk)
1. Navajo Indians—Juvenile literature. I. Title.

E99.N3B577 2015
979.1004'9726—dc23   2014041747

CCSS: RI.5.1, 2, 3, 5, 6, 8, 9; RH.6-8.4, 5, 6, 7, 8, 9

First Edition HC 9 8 7 6 5 4 3 2 1
First Edition PBK 9 8 7 6 5 4 3 2 1

PEOPLES of NORTH AMERICA

Navajo

VALERIE BODDEN

CREATIVE EDUCATION • CREATIVE PAPERBACKS

Table of Contents

A NAVAJO BOY (ON PAGE 3); ROCK ART LEFT BEHIND
IN SOUTHEASTERN UTAH BY NAVAJO, PUEBLOAN,
AND OTHER TRIBES (PICTURED HERE)

Introduction

More than 500 years ago, the Navajo established their homeland on the vast expanses of the Colorado **PLATEAU** in southwestern North America. The red-brown sands stretched hundreds of miles in every direction, dotted by spots of green—mostly sagebrush and desert grasses. Towering **MESAS** and rock formations sculpted by the wind rose over the landscape. In some places, the high land of the plateau plunged into deep canyons surrounded by steep walls of red rock. Yucca, piñon, and juniper grew in these canyons, which were home to mountain lions, rabbits, and foxes. On the edges of the plateau, brown bears, wolves, and deer ranged over high mountains covered with forests of pine, fir, and oak. The Navajo rode their horses across this land. They knew where to farm, where to hunt, where to graze their sheep, and where to disappear into the rocks to hide when necessary.

The Navajo called their land *Dinetah*, "land of the people," and they called themselves *Diné*, or "The People." In the 1600s, Spanish explorers referred to the Diné as "Navajo." That name was likely based on a Spanish interpretation of a name given to the Diné by the local Tewa peoples. It meant "great planted fields." A new name was not all the Spanish introduced to the Navajo. They also brought horses and sheep—and with these animals came a whole new way of life. Although continued encounters with the Spanish and later dealings with American settlers threatened that way of life, it ultimately survived. Today, many Navajo continue to incorporate aspects of their traditional culture into their daily lives.

SMALLER THAN MESAS, BUTTES IN THE COLORADO PLATEAU STILL MAKE A TOWERING IMPRESSION.

· NAVAJO ·

Southwestern Arrival
⟶ PEOPLES *of* NORTH AMERICA ⟵

lthough they are today known as a southwestern tribe, the Navajo did not arrive in the Southwest until sometime between A.D. 1000 and 1500. Before that time, the ancestors of the Navajo lived far to the north, in Alaska, western Canada, and present-day California and Oregon. There they hunted caribou, moose, and bears; gathered wild nuts and berries; and caught fish. They lived in cone-shaped homes covered with bark or animal hides and traipsed through the snow using snowshoes and dogs pulling sleds.

ANTHROPOLOGISTS call these ancestral Navajo the Athapaskans because of the language they spoke, which belongs to the Athapaskan language family. Many Athapaskan-speaking peoples remained in the north. But at some point, groups of them began to move south from their homeland, perhaps because of food shortages or war with neighboring peoples. The groups likely made their way through the Rocky Mountains or along the Great Plains, stopping for periods of time and then starting again. Eventually, after traveling more than 2,000 miles (3,219 km), they reached southwestern North America.

Most of the Athapaskans moved onto lands east of the Rio Grande. They became known as the Apache. But one group settled on the Colorado Plateau,

THE ATHAPASKANS MOVED AWAY FROM THE ARCTIC LAND OF ALASKA AND ITS CARIBOU TO THE HOTTER CLIMATE OF THE SOUTHWEST.

FROM THEIR EARLIEST DAYS IN DINETAH THROUGH THE 20TH CENTURY, NAVAJO WOMEN TENDED THEIR FAMILIES' CROPS.

in the northern section of present-day New Mexico, and later spread into parts of Arizona, Utah, and Colorado. They soon became known as the Navajo.

Although they had arrived in a new land, the Navajo continued to live as hunters and gatherers. They may have begun to plant small gardens, too, using agricultural techniques they had picked up on their long journey south. Soon, though, the Navajo began to farm more extensively, taught by the **PUEBLOAN** peoples who lived around them. Navajo farmers began to raise fields of corn, squash, and beans. As the Navajo and Pueblo interacted more frequently, the Pueblo influenced Navajo crafts and religion as well.

Although the Navajo adopted many aspects of Puebloan culture, relations between the groups varied from friendly to hostile. They worked together to defeat the Spanish in battle in 1680, for example. But when the Pueblo later allied themselves with the Spanish, they became the target of frequent Navajo raids. Navajo relations with the Utes to the north and the Comanche to the east were generally unfriendly. The Utes, especially, often raided the Navajo. But on many occasions, the Navajo allied with some of the Apache tribes who lived to the south and east.

When they weren't fighting, the Navajo and Pueblo were trade partners. The Navajo provided the Pueblo with meat, hides, and salt in return for goods such as cotton cloth and metal tools obtained from the Spanish. In the 1600s, the Pueblo introduced the Navajo to horses and sheep brought by the Spanish. The Navajo traded for these animals. Or, more often, they obtained them by raiding Pueblo or Spanish herds. Soon, the Navajo had adopted the lifestyle of shepherds.

When they moved to the Southwest, the Navajo began to live

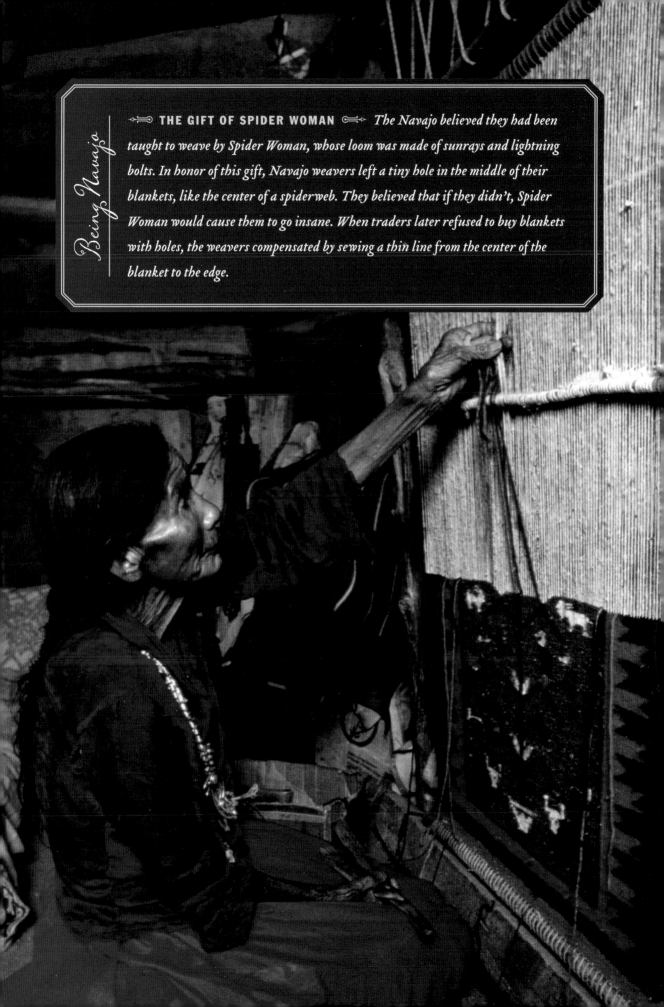

THE GIFT OF SPIDER WOMAN

The Navajo believed they had been taught to weave by Spider Woman, whose loom was made of sunrays and lightning bolts. In honor of this gift, Navajo weavers left a tiny hole in the middle of their blankets, like the center of a spiderweb. They believed that if they didn't, Spider Woman would cause them to go insane. When traders later refused to buy blankets with holes, the weavers compensated by sewing a thin line from the center of the blanket to the edge.

in a new kind of shelter called a hogan. The earliest hogans were
made by arranging three poles in a triangle shape so that they met
at the top. Smaller poles and branches were leaned against the
three poles to make a cone-shaped structure that was then covered
with mud. An opening was left for a door, and a small hole might
be left in the top to let smoke out, but there were no windows. The
entrance was usually covered with a blanket. Some later hogans
were six-sided, with dome-shaped roofs. Some were made of stone
instead of logs. No matter how they were constructed, hogans
were ideal shelters for Dinetah, as they remained cool in the summer and warm in the winter. Plus, they were easy to keep clean.

The hogan was more than just a home to the Navajo. It was
also considered a holy place, since the Navajo believed its design
had been given to them by gods known as the Holy People. The
round shape of the hogan symbolized another god, the Sun, and
the door of a hogan always faced east, toward the sunrise. After
construction of a hogan was completed, the people gathered to
hold a ceremony, in which the home was sprinkled with corn pollen and prayers were offered to "let this place be happy."

Inside, a hogan had only one room. Family members slept on

⟜⟞ FEAR OF DEATH ⟜⟞ *The Navajo were afraid of all things related to death. Whenever someone died, his family quickly buried or burned his body so that his spirit couldn't come back to torment them. If the person died in a hogan, the Navajo knocked a hole in the structure's north wall to get the body out. That hogan was then abandoned in favor of a new home. Later, when traders moved onto the Navajo reservation, they took on the role of burying the Navajo dead.*

sheepskin bedding, which was tucked away in trunks along with clothing when not in use. Other items were hung on the walls or from the roof. If a family needed more space, additional hogans might be built nearby for older children or for storage.

Most families also built a ramada for use in the summer. Ramadas were rectangular-shaped shelters with a roof and walls made of branches. One or two sides of the ramada might be left open to the air. The ramada shaded the Navajo from the sun but allowed cooling breezes to reach them. The women used the ramada as a place in which to cook or weave, and families sometimes slept there as well.

Most Navajo families had hogans in more than one location because they traveled with their sheep to different pastures throughout the year. They might have a summer hogan in the lowlands, where there was enough water for farming, and a winter hogan at a slightly higher elevation, where it would be easier to get firewood. The 2 sites might be up to 40 miles (64.4 km) apart.

The Navajo generally built their hogans in small family clusters. The cluster was usually centered around the oldest female in the family, called the "head mother," and her husband. Nearby

The fertility god Kokopelli is commonly featured in rock art (opposite) and handmade items of Southwestern tribes (above).

were the hogans of their unmarried adult children as well as the homes of their married daughters, who lived with their husbands and children.

In addition to being part of an extended family group, every Navajo individual belonged to a clan. The members of all the clans considered themselves to be part of a larger family descended from the same ancestor. Clan members were spread widely across Dinetah, and some members might never even meet. But when they did encounter other members of their own clan, the Navajo treated them with special care. All Navajo children became a member of their mother's clan at birth. And because clan members were considered related, they were not allowed to intermarry. A Navajo could not marry someone from his or her father's clan, either.

No matter where they lived, all Navajo considered Dinetah sacred, and they thought of themselves as being part of the world around them. Four mountains marked the borders of their land: *Sis Naajini* (Blanca Peak) in the east, *Doo ko' oosliid* (San Francisco Peaks) in the west, *Tso dzilh* (Mount Taylor) in the south, and *Dibe Nitsaa'* (Hesperus Peak) in the north. The Navajo believed that, as long as they remained in this "land between four mountains," their gods would continue to bless them.

For most of their history, the Navajo people did not have a central government. Instead, they were split into small groups called outfits. An outfit was usually made up of 2 or more extended family clusters and had a population of 20 or 30 people. A large outfit might have more than 100 members. The families of an outfit were generally related and lived in the same basic area, though their hogans might be far apart. They came together to share farming and herding tasks as well as to hold ceremonies. Each outfit was led by a *naat'aanii*, or headman, who ruled by **CONSENSUS**. Any members of the outfit who disagreed with him could choose to ignore him or to move to a different group.

Only occasionally did the various headmen throughout Dinetah come together in a council called a *naachid*. Here they might discuss important issues—such as war with outsiders—that affected all the Navajo people. But even the decisions of the naachid were not binding, and a local outfit could choose not to follow them.

For the Navajo, warfare generally meant conducting raids for horses and sheep. Their most common targets were the Pueblo and the Spanish. For three days before a raid, the men of the raiding party participated in sweat baths,

ALTHOUGH FAMILIES MOVED FROM PLACE TO PLACE—USUALLY FOLLOWING HERDS—HORSES MADE DESERT TRAVEL EASIER.

NAVAJO FARMERS PLANTED NEAR WATER SOURCES AND LEARNED HOW TO DIVERT THAT WATER TO NOURISH CROPS.

prayers, and ceremonies. When it was time to set out, they put on shirts made of several layers of buckskin to stop enemy arrows. They carried bows and arrows as well as spears, war clubs, and knives. They might spend many days traveling to their target. When they arrived, they attacked just as the sun came up, riding into the enemy's pasture and driving out hundreds of sheep.

The men may have acquired the sheep, but the women cared for the herds, which were considered her property. While the sheep provided a reliable source of meat, most families did not own a large enough herd to live only by raising livestock. Most continued to plant fields in the canyon bottoms each summer. Then they would move away to find new grazing land for the sheep. In the fall, a few members of the family would return to harvest the crops, as the rest remained with the sheep.

Along with farming and raising livestock, the Navajo gathered wild foods such as piñon nuts, acorns, sunflower seeds, wild potatoes, and cactus fruits. Men also hunted, sometimes singly but often in groups of up to 10. Some animals, such as the black-tailed deer, pronghorn, brown bear, and golden eagle were considered sacred. The Navajo could not hunt these animals unless they performed specific rituals before, during, and after the hunt. Other animals, such as mule deer, bighorn sheep, mountain lions, and turkeys, did not require ritual preparation to hunt.

Navajo hunters carried bows and arrows, spears, and traps. Later, they used rifles as well. In some cases, they wore deer or antelope masks and crept up on the animals. At other times, they

WHAT'S IN A NAME? *Shortly after birth, a Navajo child was named by his parents. But this name was not told to anyone else. The child's parents didn't even use the name, since it was considered his personal property. Instead, if people wanted to talk about the person to someone else, they used a nickname. Nicknames might change several times throughout the person's life. But this didn't matter to the Navajo. Whenever they addressed one another, they used a kinship term (such as "brother" or "cousin")   or "my friend."*

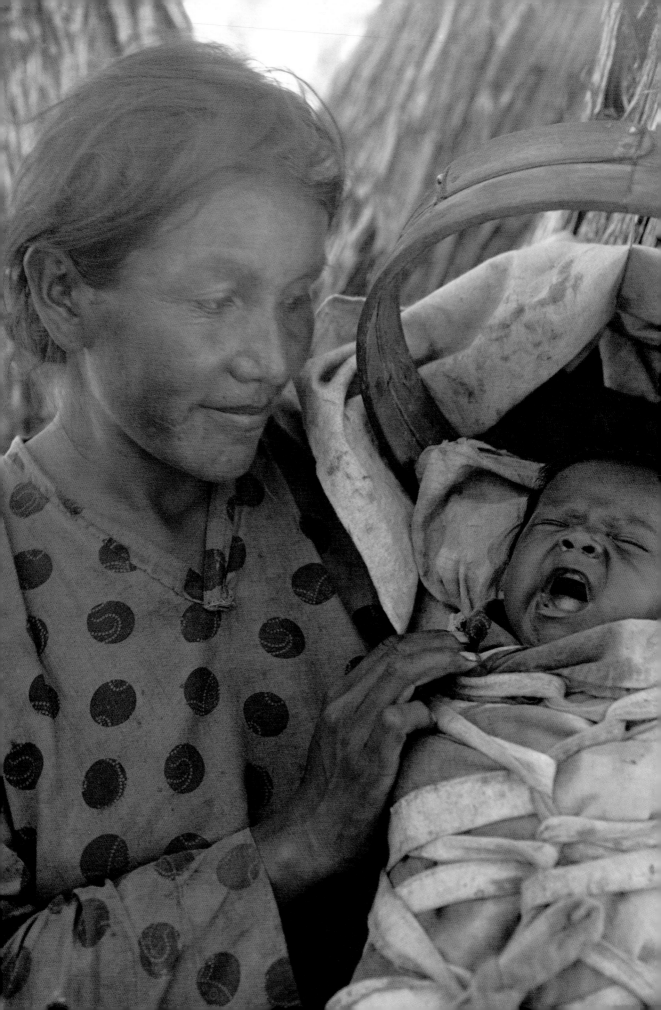

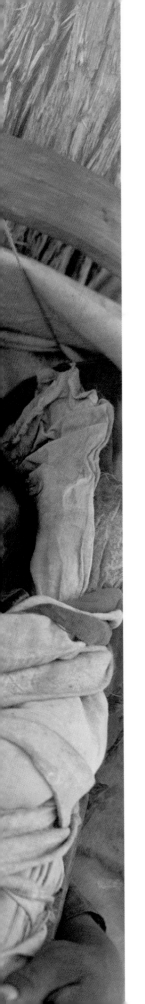

formed a circle around prey such as rabbits, then moved in to trap the animals in the middle, where they could be clubbed.

Women generally cooked their family's food. They also took care of the children. Infants were usually kept in a **CRADLEBOARD**, which a mother could prop up nearby while she worked. Or she could strap it on her back when riding her horse. Young children learned by observing and imitating. By the time they were five, most children had been given a lamb to care for. Young boys were taught to hunt and track, while girls learned to weave.

Weaving was an important part of every Navajo woman's life. After shearing her sheep and cleaning and spinning the wool, a woman used a vertical loom to weave the wool into blankets. The Navajo used the blankets in their hogans and under the saddles of their horses. In addition, women stitched two blankets together to make a dress, while men wore the blankets over their shoulders. In the winter, both men and women wore the blankets as serapes, or shawls. Navajo blankets were widely admired by the Spanish and Americans, who often traded for them. One Spanish official noted that the blankets had "more delicacy and taste" than those of European weavers.

While the women wove, Navajo men learned the trade of silversmithing. Beginning in the 1800s, they melted down silver coins and fashioned the metal into jewelry, belts, buttons, and bells. Eventually, they began inlaying their silver goods with turquoise. Like Navajo blankets, the silver items were in high demand among Spanish and American traders.

As they went about the tasks of their daily life, the Navajo were always aware of the spiritual world. In fact, religion was so much a part of their everyday lives that they didn't have a separate word for it. The Navajo believed in many gods. Among the most important were the Holy People, including Changing Woman, who

NOT ONLY A MEANS OF CARRYING BABIES, CRADLEBOARDS ALSO HELPED PROTECT INFANTS FROM SUN AND PESTS.

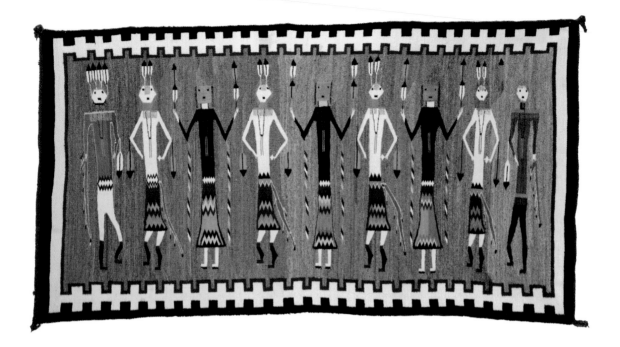

was said to have created people, and her husband Sun. Changing Woman was always good, but the other Holy People could cause both good and evil. Other spirits called Yeis represented natural forces that could be called upon during healing ceremonies.

The Navajo believed it was necessary to maintain a state of harmony in the universe. They called this state of harmony *hózhó*, and they preserved it in their daily lives by singing, chanting, or saying prayers as they went about their work. Hózhó was also maintained or restored through more than 50 special ceremonies. A ceremony was conducted by a *hataali*, or singer. Almost all singers were men, and each knew only two or three ceremonies by heart, since a single ceremony might involve hundreds of songs and rituals.

Usually, a ceremony was held for someone who was ill or who had encountered other evils, such as a dead body or lightning, which could disturb hózhó. The ceremony might involve the subject's extended family, and sometimes more than 100 people would gather for the ceremony's conclusion. Some ceremonies lasted up to nine days.

⟜⟞ **BECOMING A SINGER** ⟜⟞ *Any boy who wanted to become a hataali, or singer, could do so by paying a more experienced singer to teach him the necessary songs and rituals. Over the course of six or seven years, he observed the older singer and then assisted him in ceremonies. Once he became a singer, the boy would be paid for his services to the people—usually with a live or butchered sheep. Occasionally, singers were accused of misusing their ceremonial knowledge to practice witchcraft and cast curses.*

In addition to singing and praying, for most ceremonies the singer or his assistants created drypaintings, sometimes called sandpaintings. Drypaintings were made by sprinkling sand, pollen, cornmeal, flower petals, ground charcoal, and brightly colored minerals on the ground to create intricate designs. A drypainting could cover 9 to 400 square feet (0.8–37.2 sq m). When it was complete, the subject sat in the middle of it. The Navajo believed that this transferred the power of the Holy People to him or her.

The most important Navajo ceremony was called the Blessing Way. Variations of the Blessing Way were used to ask the Holy People to bless a new home or marriage, provide help during childbirth, or protect warriors from danger. Other important rituals included the Enemy Way, which was usually performed after a person had injured or killed someone in war, and the Night Way, to help someone who was blind or paralyzed.

IN A RITUAL SPANNING MULTIPLE DAYS, SEVERAL DRYPAINTINGS MAY BE CREATED TO SERVE DIFFERENT PURPOSES.

In the 1520s, Spanish explorers began to march through present-day Mexico, claiming the land for Spain. Soon, they forged north into the American Southwest. The first known contact between the Spanish and the Navajo was in 1583, when an expedition led by Spanish explorer Antonio de Espejo encountered the Navajo near Mount Taylor in what is now New Mexico. The meeting was peaceful, and the two groups even traded items.

By 1598, Spain had laid claim to New Mexico, and settlers began to arrive in the region. The Navajo were fascinated by the animals the Spanish brought, especially the horses and sheep. In the early 1600s, they began to obtain such animals for themselves, largely through raids, and soon they had transformed themselves into shepherds.

For most of the 1600s and 1700s, the Navajo continued to raid Spanish herds. They also raided herds of the Puebloan peoples, who had become Spanish allies. Through such raids, the Navajo eventually increased their own herds until their sheep populations numbered in the tens of thousands.

The raids were not one-sided—nor were they limited to livestock. The Spanish also raided the Navajo, kidnapping women and children, whom they sold as slaves to be used in the homes of wealthy Spanish landowners

NAVAJO LIVING IN CANYON DE CHELLY DOCUMENTED SUCH DAILY EXPERIENCES AS ENCOUNTERS WITH SPANISH HORSEMEN.

MANUELITO'S AG-
GRESSIVE NATURE
KEPT HIM FROM
HEEDING CALLS
FOR PEACE UNTIL
HIS HERDS WERE FI-
NALLY WIPED OUT.

and officials. The Utes and Comanche, who had allied themselves with the Spanish, also tore through Navajo lands, grabbing women and children to be sold in the slave market. At times, the raids between the Spanish and the Navajo turned into all-out warfare. The two sides declared peace several times, only to begin raiding each other again soon afterward.

In 1821, Mexico gained independence from Spain. The new government controlled not only Mexico but also the present-day states of Texas, New Mexico, Arizona, Colorado, Utah, Nevada, and California. But the change in government did little to alter the situation in New Mexico, where the Navajo and Spanish stepped up their raids on one another.

Mexican rule did not last long. In 1848, New Mexico officially passed into the hands of the United States at the end of the **MEXICAN–AMERICAN WAR**. Navajo raiders continued to strike, and, with their Apache allies, rode off with 450,000 American sheep by 1850. At the same time, slave traders in New Mexico continued to snatch Navajo women and children.

Things only got worse when American ranchers began to graze their herds on Navajo lands. In 1851, the U.S. military built Fort Defiance on Navajo grazing land just southeast of Canyon de Chelly (*SHAY*). In 1858, a Navajo headman named **MANUELITO** brought his herd to graze near the fort on land the soldiers had claimed for their own animals. When soldiers shot 60 of his animals, Manuelito was outraged. "The water there is mine, not yours, and the same with the grass," he said. "Even the ground it grows from belongs to me, not to you. I will not let you have these things." On April 30, 1860, Manuelito and 1,000 warriors attacked Fort Defiance, almost taking the American stronghold.

KIDNAPPED FOR SCHOOL ⟫ When the first schools on the Navajo reservation opened in the 1870s, most Navajo were reluctant to have their children "learn paper." This attitude was not helped by an 1887 law that allowed government agents to round up Navajo students and force them to attend boarding schools. Sometimes, the children were taken without their parents' knowledge. Students had to take "American" names, wear American-style clothing, and speak English. Those caught speaking their native language were beaten.

The American response was swift, with U.S. soldiers, New
Mexican **MILITIAS**, and allied Utes marching through Dinetah. As
soldiers tracked through their land, the Navajo were forced into
hiding. Most Navajo families couldn't harvest their fields, many
of which the invaders had burned, anyway. By December, the
starving Navajo had to surrender.

In 1862, Fort Defiance was assigned a new commander,
General James H. Carleton. Carleton believed the Navajo's land
was full of gold, and he wanted access to it. He devised a plan for
a "grand experiment to make civilized human beings out of sav-
ages" by gathering them "onto a reservation away from the haunts
and hills and hiding places of their country."

Carleton picked out an empty stretch of land in eastern New
Mexico for the reservation. The Navajo had no interest in go-
ing there. "I will never leave my country," Navajo headman
BARBONCITO told Carleton, "not even if it means I will be killed."
Carleton ordered **CHRISTOPHER "KIT" CARSON**, a former **INDIAN
AGENT**, to round up the Navajo by force.

Beginning in August 1863, Carson and his men marched
through Dinetah, burning everything in their path—hogans,

⇒◦ FURS AND EVENING GOWNS ◦⇐ *In the 1940s, newspapers across the country printed articles describing conditions in the Navajo Nation. People responded by sending the Navajo gifts of food and clothing. But much of what they sent showed how little they knew about what the Indians really needed. As American anthropologist Ruth Underhill described, "It was strange to see a Navajo woman in a fur coat, mounting her horse to drive a flock of sheep. It was stranger to see the boxes of evening gowns and silver slippers."*

fields, orchards—and taking the Navajo's livestock. The Navajo retreated into the caves and crevices of the canyons, and few were caught at first. But by January 1864, the Navajo were becoming too hungry to avoid surrender any longer.

They were sorted into large groups and forced to walk to their new reservation, 370 miles (595 km) away. Most traveled on foot, struggling through strong blizzards with little food or clothing. Those who fell behind were shot. Many children were carried off by New Mexican slave raiders along the way.

After nearly 20 days on the trail, the Navajo completed what became known as their "Long Walk" and reached their new reservation, called Bosque Redondo. By March 1865, more than 9,000 Navajo had settled on Bosque Redondo's 40 square miles (104 sq km). The Americans instituted a new form of government on the reservation, appointing Barboncito as head chief, with several sub-chiefs under him.

Since Bosque Redondo offered almost no timber, most families dug holes in the ground to create rough shelters. Others hung sheepskins or cowhides from poles to block the wind. They traveled 20 miles (32.2 km) or more to find firewood, or they dug up

mesquite roots to use as fuel.

The army had not been prepared to house and feed so many people, and food supplies often ran low. The Navajo were provided with rancid bacon and flour full of bugs. In addition, the bitter water from the nearby Pecos River made many people sick. The Americans gave the Navajo seeds for farming. But four years in a row, the Navajo's crops were ruined by caterpillars, droughts, hail, or floods.

Thanks to inadequate food and shelter, the Navajo quickly fell victim to disease. Within 4 years, 2,000 Navajo died on the reservation. In addition, Bosque Redondo had been built on Comanche lands, and Comanche warriors entered the reservation freely to take Navajo animals, women, and children. The soldiers at nearby Fort Sumner could do little besides offer the Navajo a few guns to defend themselves.

The Navajo were certain their gods had deserted them as punishment for leaving their homeland. They pleaded with the Americans to let them return. In 1865, a group from Washington, D.C., was sent to examine conditions on the reservation. They were shocked by what they found. And they were worried about the cost of feeding the Navajo, which had soared to more than $2 million. But it was another three years before any action was taken. Finally, in May 1868, the federal government decided it was time to close Bosque Redondo.

The Americans at first considered relocating the Navajo to Texas or to Indian Territory in present-day Oklahoma. But Barboncito insisted, "We do not want to go to the right or left, but straight back to our own country."

On June 18, 1868, the Navajo left Bosque Redondo for good. They walked back to Dinetah in a single group that stretched for 10 miles (16.1 km) along the trail. When they finally came into sight of their homeland, they were overjoyed. "We felt like talking to the ground, we loved it so," Manuelito said, "and some of the old men and women cried with joy when they reached their homes."

The Navajo homeland was not as large as it had once been. Before they left Bosque Redondo, the Navajo had signed the Treaty of 1868, which created a 3,900-square-mile (10,101 sq km) Navajo reservation that encompassed only 10 percent of the former Navajo homeland. Over the next 3 decades, however, the size of the reservation was gradually increased, until it covered 26,000 square miles (67,340 sq km) in New Mexico, Arizona, and Utah. The government system created by the Americans at Bosque Redondo remained in place, with the head chief and sub-chiefs responsible for maintaining order.

When they returned to their homeland from Bosque Redondo, the Navajo found their fields overgrown. Most families had no livestock left, but in 1869, the government provided the Navajo with 14,000 sheep and 1,000 goats to replace those the U.S. Army had killed or stolen.

A NATIONAL MONUMENT SINCE 1931, CANYON DE CHELLY PRESERVES A PORTION OF THE NAVAJO'S ANCESTRAL HOMELAND.

RAILROAD WORK
CONTINUED TO
PROVIDE JOBS FOR
THE NAVAJO, ESPE-
CIALLY DURING THE
1940S WAR YEARS.

In the 1880s, the railroad came to the reservation. Although railroads took over some of the Navajo's best lands, they also created jobs for many Navajo men. And trains brought traders to the reservation. The traders offered coffee, sugar, and manufactured goods in return for wool, sheepskin, livestock, and woven blankets. They also served the Navajo as interpreters, bankers, postmasters, and even gravediggers.

With trade flourishing, the Navajo prospered. By 1900, their population had reached 20,000. Among them, Navajo shepherds owned more than a million sheep. In the 1920s, a new source of wealth came to the Navajo, as oil was discovered on the reservation. A new government in the form of a tribal council was created to negotiate deals with oil companies.

Then, in the 1930s, U.S. government officials began to express concerns about soil erosion from overgrazing on Navajo lands. Some officials feared that **SILT** from the reservation would wash into the Colorado River and clog the reservoir behind the recently built Hoover Dam. Laws were passed limiting the number of sheep and goats each Navajo family could own. The Navajo had to sell their "surplus" animals—numbering in the thousands—to government officials, who bought them at low prices. Sometimes, the animals were slaughtered and left to rot as the Navajo, who no longer had enough sheep to earn a living, went hungry. The Navajo were devastated, but they were powerless to stop the destruction. A Navajo man named Martin Johnson later described the experience: "There was blood running everywhere in the corral as we just stood there and watched. [My wife] ... cried about her goats as they were killed. Then we just left to go back home."

Being Navajo

→═══ **TALKING IN CODE** ═══← *Because the Navajo language was unknown to America's enemies in World War II, it became a perfect code. But the language lacked words for many aspects of the modern military. So the code talkers made some substitutions. For "submarine," they used the word* besh-lo, *meaning "iron fish," while they referred to "fighter plane" as* dah-he-tih-hi, *or "hummingbird." The contributions of the Navajo code talkers were largely kept secret until the 1990s. In 2001, the code talkers were awarded* CONGRESSIONAL GOLD MEDALS.

Despite their anger over herd reduction, when the U.S. entered World War II, 3,600 Navajo joined the U.S. military. About 420 of them served in the war against Japan as "code talkers." They used their native language as a code to pass secret information from one American base to another. Thousands of Navajo back in the U.S. also helped the war effort by taking jobs in the defense industry.

When the Navajo men returned to their reservation after the war, they found things in a state of disrepair. The people were starving, and about 10 percent of the population suffered from **TUBERCULOSIS**. The reservation had fewer than 100 miles (161 km) of paved roads. Few people had jobs, and schools had been abandoned. By the late 1940s and early 1950s, government funding helped the Navajo build new roads, hospitals, and schools.

After the war, the Navajo also turned to a new natural re-source to bring wealth to the reservation. Throughout the 1950s, more than 1,000 **URANIUM** mines were opened across the res-ervation. Hundreds of Navajo men went to work in the mines, but they were not told of the risks of radiation exposure from working with uranium. By 1970, nearly 200 Navajo miners had died of cancer and other radiation-related illnesses. Although the mines began to close in the late 1960s, radioactive waste was left in huge piles—up to 70 feet (21.3 m) high and a mile (1.6 km) long. Children played on the piles, and radioactive dust blew across the reservation and contaminated its water supply. The sand was also mixed into cement that was used to build houses on the reserva-tion. Cleanup efforts began early in the 21st century, but the U.S. Environmental Protection Agency predicted that it would take several decades before all the abandoned mines had been properly cleaned up.

The uranium mines weren't the Navajo's only problem, though. After the return from Bosque Redondo, many Navajo had

COAL MINING NEAR THE NAVAJO NATION'S CAPITAL OF WIN-DOW ROCK PROVED MODERATELY SAFER THAN DEALING WITH URANIUM.

FROM SILVERSMITH-
ING (ABOVE) TO
DANCING (OP-
POSITE), MODERN
NAVAJO KEEP
TRADITIONAL ART
FORMS ALIVE.

settled on lands that the U.S. had promised to the Hopi, a Pueblo tribe. Although the Navajo and Hopi had lived together on these lands for nearly 100 years, in 1974, the U.S. government passed a law requiring 10,000 Navajo and about 100 Hopi to move. Most Navajo living in the area were resettled in cities off the reservation, where many had difficulty adjusting. Some Navajo simply refused to move, and in 1996, the Hopi agreed to grant them a 75-year lease to remain on the land. By 2012, a few Navajo families still refused to either move or sign a lease, insisting that the land belonged to their people.

Today, more than 300,000 Navajo people live within the borders of the Navajo reservation, known as the Navajo Nation. Many others live near the reservation, but some Navajo make their homes as far away as Los Angeles or Kansas City, Missouri.

Those living on the reservation continue to observe traditional Navajo practices. Some still live in hogans, and even those who live in more modern-style houses often build a hogan next door

⇌ **A NUCLEAR DISASTER** ⇌ *On July 16, 1979, the Navajo Nation became the site of one of the worst radioactive disasters in U.S. history. Radioactive waste spilled from a holding pond at a uranium mine near Gallup, New Mexico. More than 100 million gallons (378.5 million l) of radioactive water rushed into the Puerco River, carrying 1,000 tons (907 t) of radioactive waste with it. The governor of New Mexico refused to seek federal disaster assistance, and cleanup proceeded slowly, continuing into the 2000s.*

for traditional ceremonies. Some hospitals on the reservation include special rooms for conducting ceremonies as well. Many Navajo people also continue to speak their native language. And Navajo-made blankets and silver are still in high demand.

THOSE WHO WISH TO MAINTAIN A CONNECTION TO THE PAST—AND TO THEIR OWN UPBRINGING—RESIDE IN HOGANS.

The Navajo people realize that holding on to their past helps ensure their future. Even as Navajo writer Charles Morgan encouraged his people to study and prepare for the future, he urged them, "Don't forget the land and the people who went before you. They will be your blessing and will make you strong." The life of the Navajo has changed much in the past 1,000 years. From their early days in the far north to their days of raiding and being raided in the American Southwest, and from their forced relocation to their return home, the Navajo have adapted to the world around them while remaining firmly rooted in their own culture.

During the winter, the Navajo spent cold nights in their hogans, telling traditional stories. These stories helped to explain the world around them. Most featured Navajo deities, such as the Hero Twins named Monster Slayer and Child Born of Water. In this story, the Hero Twins save the people from the monsters that keep bothering them.

Monster Slayer and Child Born of Water were worried about their people. They wanted to stop the monsters from hurting them. They decided to ask their father to help them destroy the monsters. But first, they had to learn who their father was. They asked Spider Woman. She told them that their father was the Sun but that they would have to go on a dangerous journey to reach him. She taught them special chants to keep them safe on the journey. She also gave them magical eagle feathers to help them along the way.

As they traveled to Sun's house, the twins met the dangers Spider Woman had told them about: Reeds That Cut, Moving Sand, and Wash That Swallows. They got past the dangers by using the chants Spider Woman had taught them. Then they came to Canyon That Closes In. The walls of the canyon started to slide in toward them, but the twins couldn't remember the chant that would save them. They pulled out their eagle feathers, which carried them up out of the canyon.

Finally, the twins reached the place called Darkness. They knew their father's house was just beyond it, so they passed through the Darkness. The doors of Sun's house were guarded by Giant Snake, Huge Black Bear, Big Thunder, and Big Wind. These guards wanted to kill the boys, but Spider Woman had taught the twins chants to get past them as well.

Finally, the twins were inside Sun's house. But their father was not home. His wife was afraid that Sun would not recognize the boys and would kill them. She hid them in clouds. But when Sun came home, he demanded to see the boys. He tested them to find out if they were really his children. He sent them into a sweat lodge that was too hot to survive, fed them poisoned corn, and threw them against a wall of knives. The boys survived the tests. Then Sun realized they were his children.

Sun asked the boys what they wanted. They said they needed a way to kill the monsters. So Sun gave them weapons. To Monster Slayer he gave Lightning That Strikes Crooked. Child Born of Water was given Lightning That Strikes Straight. The boys used their lightning to kill many monsters, including He Who Kicks Them Off Cliffs, Horned Monster, Monster Bird, and Eyes That Kill. The monsters they killed turned into huge stones, which can still be seen rising over the Navajo's lands today.

ANTHROPOLOGISTS
people who study the physical traits,
cultures, and relationships of different
peoples

BARBONCITO
(c. 1820–71) Navajo singer and headman
who eluded Kit Carson's forces for a time
but was captured and forced to relocate
to Bosque Redondo; appointed head chief
of the Navajo by the U.S. government,
he signed the Treaty of 1868 creating the
Navajo reservation

CHRISTOPHER "KIT" CARSON
(1809–68) American explorer who guided
military expeditions to the western U.S.;
he served as an Indian agent to the Ute and
in 1863 led the roundup of the Navajo to
send them to Bosque Redondo

CONGRESSIONAL GOLD MEDALS
the highest honors awarded by Congress for
outstanding service or achievement

CONSENSUS
agreement by all or most of a group

CRADLEBOARD
a board or frame to which an infant could
be strapped to be carried on the back

INDIAN AGENT
someone assigned to deal with specific
Indian tribes on the government's behalf

MANUELITO
(c. 1818–94) Navajo headman who led an
attack on Fort Defiance in 1860 and hid
from Kit Carson's roundup for two years
before surrendering and moving to Bosque
Redondo; in 1870, he was appointed head
chief

MESAS
flat, raised areas of land with steep sides

MEXICAN–AMERICAN WAR
fought from 1846 to 1848 between the
U.S. and Mexico over Texas, the conflict
resulted in the U.S. gaining control over the
lands of the American Southwest

MILITIAS
armies made up of citizens instead of
professional soldiers

PLATEAU
a high, flat expanse of land

PUEBLOAN
having to do with the Pueblo Indians, who
lived in the American Southwest in large,
flat-roofed housing complexes

SILT
tiny pieces of dirt, rock, and sand that often
collect on the bottoms of bodies of water

TUBERCULOSIS
a contagious disease that causes fever,
cough, and difficulty breathing

URANIUM
a hard, silver-colored, radioactive metal
used as fuel in nuclear power plants and
nuclear weapons

Brown, Dee. *Bury My Heart at Wounded Knee: An Indian History of the American West.* New York: Sterling, 2009.

Cassidy, James, ed. *Through Indian Eyes: The Untold Story of Native American Peoples.* Pleasantville, N.Y.: Reader's Digest, 1995.

Hoxie, Frederick E., ed. *Encyclopedia of North American Indians.* Boston: Houghton Mifflin, 1996.

Josephy, Alvin M. Jr. *500 Nations: An Illustrated History of North American Indians.* New York: Knopf, 1994.

Lindig, Wolfgang. *Navajo.* New York: Facts on File, 1993.

Locke, Raymond Friday. *The Book of the Navajo.* 5th ed. Los Angeles: Mankind, 1992.

Time-Life editors. *People of the Desert.* Alexandria, Va.: Time-Life Books, 1993.

Trimble, Stephen. *The People: Indians of the American Southwest.* Santa Fe, N. Mex.: School of American Research, 1993.

READ MORE

King, David C. *The Navajo.* New York: Benchmark, 2006.

Marcello, Patricia Cronin. *The Navajo.* San Diego: Lucent, 2000.

WEBSITES

AMERICAN SOUTHWEST VIRTUAL MUSEUM
http://swvirtualmuseum.nau.edu/gallery3/index.php/
Learn more about the world of the Navajo with pictures of places and artifacts.

NATIONAL MUSEUM OF THE AMERICAN INDIAN: NATIVE WORDS, NATIVE WARRIORS
http://nmai.si.edu/education/codetalkers/
Learn more about the code talkers and how they helped the U.S. military during World War II.